EIGHT KEYS
TO
COMMUNICATE
BETTER

André Bustanoby

PYRANEE
BOOKS

Zondervan Publishing House
Grand Rapids, Michigan

Eight Keys to Communicate Better

This is a Pyranee Book
Published by the Zondervan Publishing House
1415 Lake Drive, S.E., Grand Rapids, Michigan 49506

This book is excerpted from *Just Talk to Me* by André and Fay Bustanoby, copyright © 1981 by The Zondervan Corporation.

Library of Congress Cataloging in Publication Data

Bustanoby, André.
    Eight Keys to communicate better.

    "Pyranee Books."
    "This book is excerpted from Just talk to me by André and Fay Bustanoby"—T.p. verso.
    1. Communication in marriage. 2. Interpersonal relations.
I. Bustanoby, André. Just talk to me. II. Title.
HQ734.B934   1985   646.7'8   85-14199
ISBN 0-310-22182-X

Unless otherwise indicated, the Scripture text used is the *New American Standard Bible*, copyright © 1960, 1962, 1963, 1968, 1971, 1972 by the Lockman Foundation, La Habra, California.

Printed in the United States of America

85 86 87 88 89 90 / 10 9 8 7 6 5 4 3 2 1

Contents

1

The Eight Issues
We Need To Talk About

Marriage and family therapists are often asked, "What are the major issues that people fight over? Are they money, sex, in-laws, child rearing, or what?"

All of these are major problems. But I prefer to look at the issues in terms of the "emotional stakes" that are involved. People argue over a variety of things but are not always aware of the larger psychological climate and the feelings that relatively innocent topics touch.

For example, a wife may become very emotional over what appears on the surface to be a rather minor thing. It may seem to her that her husband tends to come home from work when he's ready instead of according to a schedule. He also pursues his own activities as he pleases without much attention to her wants. He lives his life quite independently of her. He asks himself if this is enough to get emotional over? Yes, if we see the real issue for what it is: centricity.

She is asking the question, "Am I important?" The question of her importance to her husband carries big emotional stakes, so big that she often wonders, "If I'm really not important to him, why should I stay in this marriage?"

I don't mean to imply that the relationship is the only thing that we need to talk about. Sometimes we need to discuss a certain *topic*, sometimes *personal* matters that concern someone else and at other times the *relationship* of the husband and wife. But the eight issues we will discuss are all related to the husband/wife *relationship*. This is where we have our greatest difficulty in communication.

The Issues

George Bach and Yetta Bernhard discuss "psychological issues" in their book *Aggression Lab.*** They suggest that there are at least eight issues that carry high emotional stakes

***Bach and Bernhard, *Aggression Lab* (Dubuque, Ia.: Kendall, Hunt Publishing Co., 1971) 25.

for couples who would communicate effectively. They are *distance, power struggle, trust, self-identity, sex, centricity, unrealistic illusions and expectations,* and *territorial aggression.* It's amazing what a different perspective we gain when we see the issues in terms of the "emotional stakes." Let's take a look at each of these issues and see what we can discover.

Distance. Every couple needs to establish a distance they feel comfortable with. This involves both *physical closeness* and *how much time* is spent together. Most couples don't find too much problem with actual physical closeness, though this can be a problem. A wife may want cuddling from her husband, but when he always takes her affection as an invitation to sex, she may become irritated. Women can distinguish between the need to be cuddled and the need for sex, though sometimes these needs go together.

More frequently, problems arise over how much closeness they have or how much time they have together. Often, a wife will complain that she doesn't have enough time with her husband. He, on the other hand, may complain that he doesn't have enough time for himself and his interests. And when he tries to take this time, his wife feels rejected. Feeling cut out, she may attempt to narrow the distance by trying to get closer to her husband. He may respond to that move by stepping up his bid for privacy until a vicious circle of negative reinforcement sets in—each does something that provokes a negative response in the other.

One wife complained to me that her husband never wanted to do things with her. To that he replied, "I feel as if she's smothering me. I need some time for myself." The issue was not that her husband didn't love her— something that could have been argued endlessly. The issue was distance comfortable to both. Here's where both can win. The wife gives her husband comfortable distance when he needs it in exchange for times of closeness that she needs.

I should not make it sound, however, that the wife is always the close-binding one. In my counseling practice I frequently run into the possessive male whose primary problem is his wife's desire for activity apart from him— both in work and play. He tends to regard her as a possession that ought to stay put at home. And when she doesn't stay put, he feels insecure. He likes all his possessions in their place so he can feel free to do what he wishes.

One of the notable things about this kind of male is that he really doesn't want his wife home so he can be with her. Often, when she does stay home, he will go out by himself or with his friends without her. This is why I say that he treats her like a possession—a thing— so that, when it's in its place, he can feel secure in going about his own business.

The issue of distance is one that must be settled to the satisfaction of each. Couples may try arm-twisting methods, complete with appropriate quotations from Scripture (men are usually guilty of using the "submission" passages), but this is no way to pursue a solution. Each must understand the other's needs. Each needs to send "I" messages on the subject and "active-listen." Only then will each discover what the other feels is a comfortable proximity. Once you discover that, you're in a position to propose a change that will work.

Power Struggle. The second issue that creates lots of problems in communication is "power struggle." This issue has to do with who calls the shots in the marriage. Does the husband always make the decisions or does the wife have a clearly defined area of responsibility in which she may make decisions? Who defines situations? For example, was the husband flirtatious with Marlene at the party as his wife claims, or was he merely being sociable as he claims? Is the situation always as he sees it, or is she allowed to disagree and define the situation differently—and have the definition stick? For example, when he socializes with his business friends, is it business as he claims, or pleasure as she claims?

Often, when couples argue over everything and anything, they should consider the possibility that neither can tolerate the idea of giving in to the other. The notable thing about a power struggle is not *what* a couple argues over; it's that they seem to argue over *everything*. If there is a possibility for a difference of opinion, they will find it.

In a marriage of equals there should be a mutual respect and balance where each shares the responsibility of defining the situation. Let me give several examples. Is the husband thoughtless [the wife's definition], or is the wife too sensitive [the husband's definition]? Is their daughter rebellious and disobedient [the wife's definition] or just a normal teenager [the husband's definition]? In reality *both* may be wrong, or there may be some truth in the way each defines the situation. But is each willing to explore the other's definition of the situation?

Christian couples who don't have a balanced view of the headship of the husband will often put the wife in the position where she is to have no opinions, and her view is never the correct view—unless it happens to agree with her husband's. Christian women who labor under a tyrannical view of headship often find themselves in conflict with what they are told by the husband and what they believe to be true.

If Ephesians 5:22–33 and 1 Peter 3:1–7 are properly applied, there need be no power struggle. God has called the woman to be a helper "suitable" for her husband (Genesis 2:18). The word translated "suitable" quite literally means "counterpart." This suggests that the woman is an equal of a different kind. As an equal in grace she is able to bring something of equal value to the relationship.

The headship of the husband does not exclude the wisdom and talent of the wife. Indeed, the husband who values his wife as his counterpart and fellow-heir will value her perspective. The woman described in Proverbs 31:10–31 is a vigorous, talented woman who engages in her own business enterprise. To be sure, it's for the benefit of the family. But she is a person in her own right.

Why, then, do couples engage in power struggles? They must honestly examine what's going on inside themselves. Is the husband still battling with an unresolved power struggle with his mother or some other significant female of the past which he continues with his wife? Is the wife still struggling with an unresolved power struggle with her father or some other significant male of the past which she still carries on with her husband?

Often the issue of self-worth is at stake. The feeling is, "If I give in to him/her, my self-worth will take a crushing blow. I will be admitting that he/she is right and I'm wrong."

Trust. The third issue is trust. Can a couple expose feelings to each other, or otherwise make themselves vulnerable, without fear of being hurt?

A couple that had argued endlessly over how much the husband should drink came to see that the issue was a deep fear in the wife that her husband would hurt her through some irresponsible act due to his drinking. One drink was enough to trigger her fear. She never knew how many more drinks would follow and lay her open to danger.

Couples often refuse to share deep feelings for fear of hurt. The husband who wants sexual relations with his wife may be afraid to ask because he is afraid of being denied. When he is denied he feels demasculinized and vulnerable. He has sexual feelings that need to be relieved, but if his wife denies him, she puts him in the position of needing sex but of having no acceptable outlet for it. Again, this can lead to a circle of negative reinforcement. He is afraid to ask because he can't trust her; she gets the impression that he has no sexual need because he doesn't ask. In such a case the issue needs to be identified. The husband may say, "Honey, I am in a bind. There are times when I want very much to have sexual relations with you, but I'm afraid to ask. I'm afraid that if I ask, you may say no, and that will leave me feeling hurt and vulnerable. I would feel that my masculinity was put down and vulnerable because I need sex, but I have nowhere to go."

Self-Identity. The fourth issue is "defense of self-identity." This becomes an issue when one spouse tries to get the other to play a role that seems foreign or unnatural. Often romantic ideals are established in courtship, and though they are unreal, each spouse tries to live up to them until the strain becomes unbearable. Then they fall into arguing about the things they don't want to do rather than dealing with the real issue—self-identity. It is being defended, and so we have conflict over it.

For example, a man may choose a woman to be his wife because she appears to be a good socializer. She seems to love parties and people. He feels that she will make the ideal hostess for his business friends. What he doesn't know is that this role is really foreign to her. She appears to be the life of the party in their courtship because she knows that this is what he wants. She actually colludes with him in establishing a false identity and a foreign role.

After years of grimly suffering through entertaining his business friends and having many fights over his expectations of her as a hostess, it finally comes out that she really does not feel comfortable in this role. The issue is not, "Who will be entertained, where, when, and how." The issue is that she is cast in the foreign role of the perfect hostess who loves parties.

I have seen this tragedy unfold in the homes of ministers and professional men such as doctors and lawyers. A woman loves a man who is planning to go into a very demanding profession. She loves him so much that she convinces herself that she will do anything for his love. If it requires socializing or many hours of separation, which are foreign to her, she may collude with her man in assuming a foreign role of socializer or strong, independent woman who can make it when her husband isn't around. After the years pass and the electric experience of courtship is a dim memory, she finds herself trapped in a role foreign to her with no way out. The way out is to identify the issue of self-identity and communicate for change.

Sex. Sex is an issue that also carries high emotional stakes but is often obscured as the real issue. Questions such as, "What kind of sex, how often, and under what conditions?" are highly relevant.

The spouse who wants to avoid sexual encounter may make excuses. The wife, for example, may become very busy with the children, attentive to their needs and home and chauffeuring them unnecessarily, so she can avoid her husband. At night or at other moments when the children are not around she may use the excuse of exhaustion. Whenever I hear a mother angrily justify the amount of time she spends on her children at the exclusion of all else, even her husband, I have a hunch that she's using them to avoid something—or someone. If she's trying to avoid her husband, then that's what they need to talk about.

Wives are not the only ones who try to avoid sex, however. Sometimes a husband may spend extra hours on the job and then come home too exhausted for sex. When the wife complains, he pulls a guilt manipulation. He says, "Here I work myself to exhaustion to give you all the things you want, and all I get is nagging."

One problem I often encounter with Christian couples is the kind of sex-play they will engage in. Sometimes the husband wants the wife to wear erotic garments and engage in sex play that she regards as distasteful. This often leads to her turning him off. She feels as if he's treating her like a Playboy bunny.

If the husband has a warped view of Christian headship he may quote 1 Corinthians 7:1-5 and tell her that it's her duty to do as he says. But if she has sex under these conditions she's ripe for a psychological reaction.

Husbands who come on like this need to be reminded that Christian husbands are to treat their wives differently than the pagans treat their wives. Paul says that sexually they are to possess the wife in "sanctification and honor" and not as the pagans did (1 Thessalonians 4:1–5). The word "sanctification" means "set apart as that which is holy." In this sense I think it has to do with making the wife feel special and treating her with the kind of deference that one does with someone special.

"Honor" is the same word used in 1 Peter 3:7, where the husband is told to assign honor to his wife as his equal, his fellow-heir of the grace of life. He hardly can treat her as a thing, a sex object, when he approaches her with this attitude.

I don't mean to imply that sex for Christians can't be fun and innovative. I'm saying that the husband's attitude toward his wife is all-important.

Centricity. Of all the issues I run into in counseling, centricity creates more problems than any other. This issue asks the question, "Am I important?" The husband who seems to have time and energy for everyone and everything other than his wife raises this question in her mind. They may argue endlessly over how he spends his time, money, and energy, but these are not the issues. The issue is that he behaves in such a way as to make his wife feel that she's low on his list of priorities.

Take, for example, the husband who is repeatedly late for dinner. His wife, attempting to fulfill her role, has a tasty dinner prepared at the usual time, and he doesn't show up. An hour later, when he does show up, he acts totally indifferent about the ruined dinner. When asked why he's late, he casually explains that he stopped off at his favorite pro shop on the way home, and time got away from him. It seems that he just couldn't decide what tennis racket was right for him.

That kind of thoughtlessness is bad enough, but suppose he acts as if the tennis racket is the biggest thing in his life. Tennis is always getting between him and his wife. She can't watch what she wants on TV because he has to watch John McEnroe. Or he can't go to his wife's favorite symphony with her because he and his buddy have planned a tennis match.

The issues they argue over aren't really the dried-out rump roast or the relative merits of symphonic music and tennis. The issue of the wife is this: "I don't feel as if I'm important enough to you for you to want to be with me—either for supper or to do with me the things I like to do."

Husbands aren't the only offenders, however. Wives raise the same question in the minds of the husbands. And the problem may be more difficult to spot when her focus is on good things such as homemaking and mothering.

Some wives are so busy trying to be good homemakers that the husband feels the house is more important than he. One husband told me, "I hate to come home at night. She has spent all day tidying up the house, and when I walk in, if I leave one thing out of place, she nails me. I realize that I should keep my things picked up, but enough is enough. I'm even afraid to get up and go to the bathroom during the night because I'm sure I'll come back and find that she has made the bed.

"And the children—everything is for the children. It doesn't seem to matter what *I* want. We must be very good parents, ever attentive to the wants and needs of the children. I think she's ruining them, being at their beck and call every moment. And all this in the name of being a good parent. Well, she can have her lovely house and her lovely children, but she can count me out. I know when I'm not wanted!"

The sad thing about this case is that the wife in question would not see that the issue was centricity. She was determined that her "selfish" husband would not keep her from being a good mother and homemaker.

Unrealistic Illusions and Expectations. This issue often goes hand in hand with the issue of self-identity. The husband may place on the wife expectations that are disappointed because she feels, "This just isn't me."

I think a lot of problems between pastors and their wives relate to this issue. Sometimes the man who enters the pastorate has certain unspoken expectations of his wife. Sometimes the church has the same expectations. But she, being unaware of these expectations, pursues her work as wife, mother, and homemaker quite unaware that she is not living up to her husband's or congregation's idea of what a good pastor's wife ought to be doing—such as playing the organ, teaching a Bible study, acting as chairman of the Ladies' Missionary Society, or whatever.

When those expectations are revealed (often in a very tense atmosphere) she feels, "Wait a minute! That just isn't me [defense of self-identity]. Why didn't you tell me that this was the name of the game before I got into it?"

I know of a pastor and his wife who tried to anticipate this problem before they accepted the call to a church. They made it clear to the church that they felt a pastor's wife was first and foremost just that—the pastor's wife, and not an assistant pastor. She would do no more or no less than any other dedicated Christian woman in the church.

Everyone said they understood, but it didn't work that way. In the six years they were at that church, some of the women repeatedly called the wife's attention to all the things the former pastor's wife did that she was not doing.

Territorial Aggression. The eighth issue is "territorial aggression." The animal kingdom demonstrates this phenomenon well. Each animal has his own "turf"—that piece of property that is his—and no other animal better step on his turf! Human beings also have their turf. It may be living space in the house, such as the husband's study, or it may be symbolic turf and symbolic aggression. For example, who drives the car when the husband and wife travel together? If she drives, does he feel that she is trespassing where she shouldn't? When they are in the car together, does he feel that his place is at the wheel? Likewise, "backseat driving" by the wife may be felt to be a form of territorial aggression by the husband. When she tells him how to drive, he may feel that she is intruding on his turf.

The wife also has her turf. She may feel that the kitchen or the laundry room is her turf. She may appear to get unreasonably angry when her husband or children mess things up, or barge in when she is working in these rooms. She may feel a personal attack because this is her turf. Generally women are very sensitive about the appearance of their homes. Society tends to regard the home as the woman's turf, and therefore how it looks is of major concern to her. She will feel, "My friends' view of me is conditioned by how my house looks. Husband and children, you better not leave it a mess!"

I'll always remember one couple who instantly resolved a terrible conflict the moment they saw this was the problem. Jim and Linda both worked outside the home, so when Jim had a day off, he thought he'd do something nice for Linda. She always seemed to feel terribly responsible for keeping the kitchen clean and good meals on the table. So he thought he'd share her burden.

The kitchen looked cluttered to him and not very efficient (he's an industrial efficiency expert by profession). He thought it needed rearranging and sprucing up.

He was quite proud of his efforts when he

finished several hours later. Linda would be delighted, so he thought, and maybe she'd also appreciate his fixing supper. He prepared a fine supper and timed it perfectly so it would be ready when Linda walked in.

At zero hour, when she walked in, he expected to be smothered with kisses for his thoughtfulness. Instead, Linda did a double-take and gave him a peck on the cheek. She was less than enthusiastic about his arrangement of the kitchen.

Jim figured she must have had a bad day. So he got on with the dinner. She acted strangely when he sat her down and served dinner. Where were the smiles and accolades?

As they ate in silence, Jim tried to figure out what was wrong. He soon found out.

Linda (playing with a vegetable on her plate): "What's this?"

Jim (tentatively): "A new recipe for zucchini."

Linda (unenthusiastically): "Oh." (She pushes the zucchini aside and tries a few bites of the roast,) "The roast sure is tough and dry."

That was it! Enough was enough! Jim uncorked. The battle that followed made the Napoleonic Wars look like an exercise in human decency. Never did they fight like that!

According to Linda, everything was wrong with the kitchen, and the meal wasn't fit for hogs. According to Jim, never did he dream that he was married to such an ingrate. Every real and imagined hurt over fifteen years of marriage roared down on them like a tornado.

Of course, the issue was territorial aggression. Though he was well-meaning, Jim had intruded onto Linda's turf.

Our turf has a lot to do with our sense of identity and our role in marriage. When someone trespasses it is a very personal matter. And when this is complicated by feelings of low self-worth, watch out!

Linda felt that Jim was implying she was not doing "her job" of homemaking to his satisfaction. In her mind he was saying "Let me show you how it ought to be done."

This was not Jim's intention. And here is a classic example of a breakdown in communication because of an inadequate understanding of feelings and intentions.

I'm happy to say that they made peace. Understanding that the issue was territorial aggression, they were able to put things in their proper perspective. People who want to make their marriage work usually respond to such insights.

Deadly Combinations of Issues

Often the issues that create problems in marriage are not just single issues. Understanding what we need to talk about can be complicated by a deadly combination of issues.

Sex and Trust. Problems relating to sex often combine with lack of trust. Husbands and wives are vulnerable when they express themselves sexually and must be able to trust each other with this sensitive part of their personhood. It's not unusual, for example, for a woman to find it difficult to be open to her husband sexually when he has been guilty of infidelity. But women are not the only ones to suffer from this deadly combination.

A client with impotency was referred to me by a doctor because the problem was not physical. The only other explanation was psychological. As we talked about the problem I explained to him that any time a man carries anger or fear into the bedroom he will have this kind of problem.

After much soul searching he identified the trouble. With tears he spilled it out.

"In all the years I've been married I've supposed that if my wife didn't meet my sexual needs I'd just leave her and find someone else. Now after twenty-five years of marriage I've come to realize that I love her so much I could never leave her—even for sex with someone else. Suddenly I felt extremely vulnerable to her. She is the only woman I will ever love—sexually or otherwise.

"When that hit me, it seemed as though she had a power over me that she never had before. That's good news and bad news. It's good because it says something about her importance to me. But it's bad because it makes me feel so vulnerable. That's the fear I'm carrying into the bedroom."

When his wife learned that this was his problem, she became a soft, warm, accepting creature. She gave him the clear message that he didn't *have to* perform sexually. She was willing to follow his lead and do whatever he wanted to do. She was so deeply touched by his love for her that it relieved him of his fear—and his problem.

Power Struggle and Unrealistic Expectations. I experienced Hank as an intense man. He cuts a fearsome figure as a man, and just talking with him was an intimidating experience. His eyes are penetrating, and he speaks with authority.

When he and Betty came for counseling, he did most of the talking. According to him, Betty had "an authority problem." By that he meant that she would not knuckle under and do what he wanted her to do. She was not being a "submissive Christian wife." He made it clear that I had a responsibility as a Christian counselor to convince her of her error.

Betty remained dutifully silent while Hank carried on the conversation and gave us a Bible lesson in how the Christian home ought to function. I had a hunch that if I let Hank go on long enough Betty would speak up. She managed to remain silent for about a half hour, but I could tell that she was having a problem with something. Finally she said, "May I say something?"

She began quietly: "Hank isn't telling the whole story. The reason we're here is that I told him we either get marriage counseling or I leave. I just got out of the hospital for surgery on my knee. Two weeks ago Hank was furious with me for not being 'submissive' and shoved me down. My leg twisted, and I tore some ligaments."

Betty continued: "This wasn't the first time. I've been manhandled before. He shoves me around a lot and has me scared to death most of the time. He's promised not to touch me again, but I'm still afraid of him."

Hank spoke up: "I know I was wrong to shove her. I won't do it again. But she must do something about her problem with my authority. She finds it difficult to submit to me."

Theirs was a case of a deadly combination of power struggle and unrealistic expectations. Because of his view of headship, Hank had some expectations of Betty that she felt were unrealistic. He expected her to give him rubber-stamp approval of everything he did. If he didn't feel like going to work, she was to go along with it. If he wanted her to pick up the children at any hour, day or night, and go off with him wherever he wanted to go, she was to do it. If they were working out in the yard and he wanted a hammer, he felt he should be able to tell her to run down to the tool shed and get it. In fact, that was one of the things that made her decide she wasn't going to let him treat her like his slave. He told her to get him a hammer, and she told him to get it himself!

This resulted in a power struggle. Because of his unrealistic expectations of her (she was to be his obedient slave) she decided that she was going to stand and fight him. The power struggle took the form of her resisting him in every way she knew how. She would not yield in any way. This, of course, was bound to be a destructive experience for both of them. But by eliminating the unrealistic expectations they were able to eliminate the need for the power struggle.

Summary. Here, then, are the eight issues we need to talk about: *distance, power struggle, trust, self-identity, sex, centricity, unrealistic illusions and expectations*, and *territorial aggression*. If you get the feeling that you really don't know what the problem seems to be in your communication, stop and see if any of these issues might be the real problem, and if not a single issue, perhaps a combination of them.

2

Communicating
for Change

In dealing with communication issues, the practical-minded couple will be looking for some techniques on "problem solving" or "negotiating differences." I call it "communicating for change," because "problem solving" seems to create an image of two people at odds with each other going grimly about the task of negotiating their differences through commercial-style bargains of the *quid pro quo* variety—"this for that."

Contracting is foreign to the spirit of this book. Couples who respect their differences and care about each other are able to talk about those differences in a spirit of good will. They can *unilaterally make changes simply because they care about each other*. The primary ingredients needed for such unilateral change are a respect for their differentness, a thorough understanding of the changes that are desired, and a desire to change and please both self and the other spouse.

Bach and Bernhard say this about contracts in *Aggression Lab:*

> "Quid pro quo"—this for that—is the basis for legal contracts. In the business world contracts are based on the *exchange* of goods or services. Please note that in the fair fight system this kind of bargaining is *not* recommended. "Equality" is a commercial value rather than an intimate reality. What is "good for the goose" in a relationship is not necessarily what is "good for the gander."
>
> Realistic intimacy flourishes better under conditions of coexistence of clearly differentiated individuals who know how to deal with their very real differences. . . . Togetherness in intimacy does not mean sameness. Consequently, the commercial definition of contracts does not apply in relationships. Unlike the business world which has money as a medium of exchange, human relationships have no way to compare and weigh the worth of behavior. We have found clinically that contracts based on the notion of bargaining—"I'll do this if you'll do that"—tend to have a much lower

probability of being fulfilled than those contracts that are in the nature of a unilateral commitment—"I will do this for you because I wish to please you."**

Premises for Communication

To help you understand what I propose in communication for change, let me list the premises this book is based on.

Respect of Differentness. Differentness can be exciting. Most people marry for complementary reasons. Only when that differentness is declared bad, wrong, or unsuitable does the complementarity become a problem. We need not think alike or act alike in marriage in order for it to work and even be exciting. But we do need to understand the scope of that differentness. We need to be able, with accurate empathy, to enter into that other person's world of pain and pleasure and to hear it, see it, think it, and feel it as he or she does. This requires an openness, one with the other, and a trust in each other that the differentness will be respected.

Any attempt at change that does not fully fathom the differentness in each other will be

**Bach and Bernhard, *Aggression Lab* (Dubuque, Ia: Kendall, Hunt Publishing Co., 1977) 25.

mechanical. There will be no true understanding of the need for change, and, because of that, enduring change is unlikely.

A Thorough Understanding of the Changes Desired. The second premise is that when differences exist as a result of differentness, a thorough understanding of the changes desired is needed. Remember, we are looking for understanding, not agreement. Those differences are to be shared in a nonattacking way through the use of "I" messages, active-listening, and shifting gears.

It's not easy to go through the process of saying or hearing painful things. Many couples would like to find a style of communication and method of change that is painless. But effective communication demands that we make constructive impact on each other. Impact that is not felt is not impact. Yes, we try to make it as nonattacking and painless as we can, but impact implies that you will feel *something*.

Effective communication for change cannot be painless, for it challenges the *status quo*—a challenge that makes all of us nervous. We tend to hang on to the *status quo* no matter how unrewarding, because it is familiar and possibly safe.

Some contracts for change are an attempt to avoid the pain of discussing differences and desires. But we just cannot approach intimacy with a commercial or legal mentality.

I am not saying that all contracts are wrong. Learning contracts or contracts for specific tasks are possible to negotiate, but they are only adjuncts to change as a unilateral decision.** A unilateral decision simply means that I am willing to change because I want to please you, and not because I'm going to get something in return. Having a pleased spouse is reward enough!

Desire to Change in Order to Please Self and Spouse. One final premise has to do with this matter of pleasing. We need a thorough understanding of our differences and the changes that are being asked. But this must occur in a context of good-will where both want to make changes that will please both spouses.

I realize, when I encourage you to send "I" messages and active-listen, that I'm asking you to open yourself to hearing things that are painful. But whether you feel damaged by what you hear or you find it a constructive step

---

**See My book *But I Didn't Want a Divorce* (Grand Rapids: Zondervan, 1978).

in the direction of change, will depend on the context you and your spouse have established. If it is a context of ill-will and you're on a "hurt hunt," it will be a damaging experience. If it is in a context of good-will, it will be painful but rewarding.

It's important to make these distinctions:

Good-will is interested in furthering the strength of the marriage.

Ill-will has no interest in furthering that bond.

Good-will sees you as a person with feelings that are to be respected.

Ill-will sees you as a "thing" to be used, or as an anonymous creature.

Without these three premises (respect of differentness, understanding of the changes desired, and willingness to please), communication for change will be impossible. You need to be able to express your desire for change in an understanding and receptive atmosphere. Communication for change that is attempted in an atmosphere of misunderstanding and distrust will not succeed. When that happens the issues that need to be addressed are misunderstanding and distrust.

Making Impact for Change

Let's suppose that you do have the proper atmosphere for change. How do you go about communicating for change? You must be able to make "impact" on your spouse. By that I mean that you must state in a straightforward and clear way what you would like to see changed and, specifically, what changes you want. You are leveling with your spouse about how you feel and what you want. Because it is done in an understanding and accepting atmosphere and in a nonattacking and nondefensive way, "impact" is not experienced as hostility.

I see eight steps in making impact for change: *Engagement, statement of the problem, feedback to the statement, request for change, feedback to the proposed change, response, rejection or acceptance,* and *planning the next engagement and closure.*

Engagement. If you wish to communicate for change your spouse must be willing to do so. Instead of jumping right in and talking to him about your need, you must ask him if he is willing to talk with you about the specific issue that bothers you. You may say, "Honey, I have a problem with the way we handle our son.

Would you be willing to talk with me about it?"

He may accept, postpone, or reject talking with you about it. Or, he may want to talk about a different issue. You want to be careful, however, that rejection or the introduction of a different issue is not a sign of communication sabotage.

My experience is that more husbands are closed to communication than their wives. They simply avoid talking about anything that might be painful. They tend to keep the discussion superficial.

If your husband refuses to engage in communication or ties up the communication in fruitless fights over what you "ought" to talk about, you have a communication saboteur on your hands. And the problem must be stated exactly that way—it is *sabotage*. You must not settle for some vague agreement that the two of you "just can't talk about your problems." You *can* if you approach it with respect of differentness, understanding, and a desire to please. But you can't if there's sabotage.

If your spouse wants to postpone the engagement, fine, but be sure to set a specific day and time to engage in your communication for change. Also, when you do engage, you may want to ask if you can follow the methodology described in this chapter. Explain that this methodology is designed to promote understanding and reduce the possibility of conflict.

Statement of Your Problem. State your problem in terms of an "I" message. "I" messages involve statements about behavior ("When I"), emotion ("I feel"), and impact ("because").

For example, the wife may say, "When I tell Mark that he can't eat anything before supper, and you permit him to do it, I feel angry and frustrated because it seems that I have no parental authority."

When this statement is made, the spouse is not to challenge it. Whether or not he thinks that he has countermanded your orders or that your parental authority is undercut by him, this *is* your view of things.

Here's where we get back to the need for a proper atmosphere for communication: There must be understanding and a desire to please. Without it, no communication of value will be possible. And if the husband refuses to understand your view of things, he is to be considered a saboteur. He need not agree with you. But with accurate empathy he must be able to see the situation through your eyes, not just his own.

Feedback to the Statement of the Problem.
Next, you need feedback from him. Did he
understand what you said in the statement of
the problem? Can he repeat it back to you?
And can he do this with an understanding
attitude?

If he tells you what you said in a tone of
voice or with an attitude that says, "You have
no right to feel that way," you have failed to
make adequate impact on him. If he does this,
he will have sabotaged the communication,
and again, it must be identified just that way:
sabotage.

Request for Change. Once you are satisfied
that he understands your point of view, you
may make a request for change. "Requesting"
is one of the best ways to bring about change
in a relationship.

In the illustration about Mark and his
mother's concern, the mother might frame her
request this way: "What I would like is for you
to respect the rules I lay down for Mark, and if
you have a difference of opinion, talk with me
privately about it." She is not asking that her
word always be law, but that they work together as a parental team and not undercut each
other.

Feedback to the Request for Change.
Again, feedback is necessary. Does the husband in this illustration understand what change she is asking for? If he understands what she is asking for, he should be able to repeat it. *This does not mean that he is agreeing to the request.* It means that he understands what she wants.

This is what I call "shared meaning." Before we can have agreement we must have understanding.

In this sequence it is totally inappropriate for the husband to criticize his wife's request, demean it, or tell her that she has no right to make such a request. *Understanding* what change is desired is all important. Refusal to give adequate and accurate feedback is tantamount to sabotage and should be identified as such. It is not a matter of not being able to communicate. It is a matter of refusal to communicate; it is engaging in communication sabotage.

Response. Now it is the husband's turn. His wife wants to know, "How about it? Are you willing to do this?" She is making a request for response.

He must now decide what is in his interest. Can he make this change and still be true to himself and his own needs? He must be careful of several things at this point.

First, he must give himself time to think about the request for change. A quick "No" may indicate a spirit of ill-will and an unwillingness to do anything his wife wants. He may ask for time to think about it (see under next step).

Second, he must be careful not to derail his wife by introducing a new issue, but *let's take one thing at a time.* Let's get closure on this matter first, even if it is to turn down her request and set a date for the next engagement in which they will talk about her "harsh attitude." You cannot rush communication without running the risk of total confusion. One step at a time, please!

Third, be careful that you don't fall into bargaining—"If I go along with you on your request, then I expect you to go along with me on my thing." Remember that bargaining is foreign to the spirit of communication in a context of goodwill. You communicate because you care, not for what you are going to get out of it.

Rejection or Acceptance. The next step is rejection or acceptance. Having decided what he wants, the spouse may either reject the request for change or accept it conditionally or unconditionally. He may say, "I will do it under these conditions. . . ." In the illustration of Mark, the husband may say, "I will go along with your directives to Mark so long as we can talk about my difference of opinion the same day."

With such a procedure it is entirely inappropriate to argue that the request for change is unwise, unreasonable, or even unscriptural. To do this is to sabotage the business at hand and get tied up in the unfruitful exercise of building a case as to why it should or should not be done. The issue is, "What changes do you need, and am I able to grant them and still be true to my own needs?" In a context of good-will, each is striving to understand and please the other. This offers the very best chance for success at communicating for change.

Planning the Next Engagement and Closure. Whatever the outcome of your attempt to communicate for change, new issues are not to be introduced at this point. It would only confuse the single issue you are attempting to communicate about. If another issue is to be considered, another engagement should be planned.

Another engagement should be planned anyway to make changes in the agreement you are presently formulating. No change should be cast in concrete but should be tentative until it stands the test of time.

The time of the next engagement will depend on how soon you want to get into new issues or how long you want to give the changes you have agreed on a chance to work. You may want to take up a new issue right away and continue on. But be careful you don't overload yourselves. At any rate, both the husband and wife should agree when this will be done. But remember, *don't put it off*.

After agreement on the change and the next engagement has been set, there should be closure. That is to say, you both have agreed to a commitment to act, and that agreement is sealed by a physical expression of good-will, like a hug or kiss.

Other Considerations in Communication for Change

I asked Fay what observations she had about our methods of problem solving or communicating for change. She said half-teasingly, "I didn't know we had any problems."

As I thought about that, I realized that we

really don't—at least no big unresolved conflicts hanging over our heads. And as we talked about it, three things came into focus that we do in addition to the above.

Keep Current. We tend to keep current with each other's feelings. Every day we either check out each other or freely share our thoughts, feelings, and intentions. We know what our emotional temperature is each day, and if there are symptoms that something's wrong, we find out what it is.

Don't Rush the Process. When we are aware of what's wrong, we avoid rushing a solution. If you rush the process, you may not fully understand your own feelings or your spouse's feelings about the presenting problem. Not only that, if you take your time you may discover that the "presenting problem" is just a symptom of a deeper issue. Time will give you an opportunity to get a sharp focus on what's going on. Impatience is the enemy of good communication.

Moreover, if you give yourself time to think about the problem, you will be able to get a sharper focus on the best possible change you can make. Fay and I are planning to move to our home on the Virginia section of the Chesapeake Bay in a few years where I want to pursue my writing ministry. With just the two of us there, I feel that we will have adequate room. Fay wants to put on an addition.

I have felt that the only reason she wants an addition is to have a place to put some of our expensive furniture from our Maryland home. So I have resisted it and suggested we sell the furniture.

We have plenty of time to decide what we'll finally do and have talked about it a lot. We have considered everything from various kinds of additions to none at all.

As I hear Fay talk now, it sounds as though she wants the addition for more than a furniture showplace. She wants to do some entertaining. I'm willing now for a modest addition. But what we will eventually do is not decided yet. The important thing is that we're open to hearing what each of us feels about the matter. We're giving ourselves time for those feelings to come into sharp focus.

Emotional Imperative. Finally, I notice that we tend to look for an "emotional imperative" in what each of us wants, particularly when each of us wants something different. For example, Fay may want "A," and I may want "B." But how badly does she need "A," and how badly do I need "B"? If on a scale of one to ten I'm a six and she's an eight, I instinctively concede to her because of the greater emotional imperative.

We have found by experience that two people in good mental health will strike a balance where, over the months, each will be yielding to the other about the same number of times. One caution must be exercised, however. Both must be totally aware of their feelings and the true emotional imperative, otherwise a false signal will be given.

Rating Your Communication for Change

How well do you communicate for change? Here's a check list that may help you sort out what you do well and what you do poorly. Both the husband and wife should fill out a check list, and if a spirit of good-will prevails, they should compare their notes. They should avoid arguing over who is right and who is wrong. The purpose of comparing notes is to understand how each feels about his/her attempt to communicate for change.

Steps in communicating for change are listed in the check list with a description of what should have occurred versus what should not have occurred. A "plus," "mid," or "minus" should be checked for each item. The wife may use one color pencil, and the husband another color. Or, each may make notes on separate sheets of paper.

"Plus" (+) means that you were successful in communicating that step.

"Mid" means that you were not totally successful in achieving the goal for that step.

"Minus" (−) means that you were not successful in achieving the goal for that step.

If you are not able to get through all the steps, draw a line under the last step you completed and make a brief statement as to why you got no further. Was it communication sabotage? Lack of time? What?

Engagement

The engagement was requested with a clear request for communication about a specific issue. It was accepted or postponed to a specific time, which was later honored.

vs.

The request for an engagement was not clear. There was talk about communication but not a specific request for an engagement. The issue was not specific. It was postponed and the postponement was not honored or rejected.

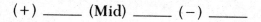(+) _____ (Mid) _____ (−) _____

Statement of Your Problem

The problem was stated as an "I" message or in a nonattacking way. It was specific. The problem was not challenged by the other spouse as invalid. The listener seemed eager to hear what the problem was.

vs.

The problem was stated in an attacking way. It was vague. It was challenged by the other spouse as invalid. The listener did not seem eager to hear what the speaker had to say and gave verbal and nonverbal messages to that effect.

(+) _____ (Mid) _____ (−) _____

Request for Change

The request for change was specific. It was received willingly. There was no verbal or nonverbal message that would discourage the speaker from making a request for change.

vs.

The request was not specific. It was not received willingly. This was seen in the rejection of the messages.

$(+)$ _____ (Mid) _____ $(-)$ _____

Feedback to the Request for Change

The spouse who received the request was able to restate the request with a respectful, nonchallenging attitude.

vs.

The spouse could not restate the request for change, or if he/she did, he/she gave the message that the speaker had no right to ask for such a change.

$(+)$ _____ (Mid) _____ $(-)$ _____

Response

The recipient of the request gave himself/herself time to think about it, did not try to derail, and avoided bargaining. The response was made in a respectful and hopeful manner.

vs.

The respondent continued to give verbal or nonverbal messages that the request was unreasonable or that he/she was refusing to respond because of the unreasonableness of the request. He/she was quick to say "No," he/she tried to derail, or he/she attempted to bargain.

(+) ____ (Mid) ____ (−) ____

Rejection or Acceptance

There was a clear acceptance of the proposed change (conditionally or unconditionally), or a rejection. Any conditions made were clear. There was no attempt to avoid accepting or rejecting the change by getting into an argument over what was requested.

vs.

The proposed change was neither accepted nor rejected; that decision was avoided. If it was accepted with condition, the conditions were not clear.

(+) ____ (Mid) ____ (−) ____

Planning the Next Engagement and Closure

If agreement was reached, a time was set to reexamine it for purposes of making any further changes. If no agreement was reached, a new engagement was set to talk about the most important issue yet unresolved. Closure was declared with a physical expression of goodwill.

vs.

Refusal to set a time for a new engagement and refusal to give closure with a physical expression of good-will.

(+) _____ (Mid) _____ (−) _____

Summary. Change that comes about through effective communication is not a "horse trade." It is a unilateral decision made in an atmosphere where there is a respect of differentness and a thorough understanding of the changes desired, and where there is a desire to change to please self and spouse.

The methodology given in this chapter is only a learning aid. Couples who communicate in a context of good-will soon learn to employ its principles as a natural part of communication for change.